PRAYERS

for Surviving
DEPRESSION

Compiled by
Kathryn James Hermes, FSP

BOOKS & MEDIA
Boston

Library of Congress Cataloging-in-Publication Data

Hermes, Kathryn.

 Prayers for surviving depression / compiled by Kathryn James Hermes

   p. cm.

 Includes bibliographical references.

 ISBN 0-8198-5952-4

 1. Prayer—Catholic Church. 2. Prayers. 3. Depression, Mental—Religious aspects—Christianity. I. Title.

 BV215.H52 2004

 242'.4—dc 22

                          2004009463

Unless otherwise noted, the Scripture quotations contained herein are from the *New Revised Standard Version Bible: Catholic Edition,* copyright © 1993 and 1989 by the Division of Christian Education of the National Council of the Churches of Christ in the U.S.A. Used by permission. All rights reserved

Cover photo: © 2003 Dynamic Graphics, Inc.

Interior photos: Mary Emmanuel Alves, FSP

All rights reserved. No part of this book may be reproduced or transmitted in any form or by any means, electronic or mechanical, including photocopying, recording, or by any information storage and retrieval system without permission in writing from the publisher.

"P" and PAULINE are registered trademarks of the Daughters of St. Paul

Copyright © 2004, Daughters of St. Paul

Published by Pauline Books & Media, 50 Saint Pauls Ave., Boston, MA 02130-3491. Printed in the U.S.A.

www.pauline.org

Pauline Books & Media is the publishing house of the Daughters of St. Paul, an international congregation of women religious serving the Church with the communications media.

4 5 6 7 8 9 10   13 12 11 10 09 08

To Bessy, Pauline, and Carissa
and all those who struggle to find
the Light in the darkness.

Contents

Invitation

Those who suffer from depression know best how difficult it can be to pray. When you are suffering with depression, it can seem impossible to muster any energy, interest, or motivation to invest in prayer. At times God seems so far away, it appears useless to try to get God's attention. "And he probably doesn't care anyway," we can conclude.

The very fact, however, that you are reading this book indicates that you desire to pray, and, even more, that God desires to give himself to you.

This book is meant to be a prayerful companion to you during your experience of depression. While you are suffering with depression, you may not be able to "pray" the way you would like or the way you think you should. Remember, even your desire to pray is prayer.

During your experience of depression, your prayer will be different from your prayer at other times in your life. God may all of a sudden seem to have disappeared. If your depression follows on an illness, the death of a loved one, or an accident, you may feel God has betrayed you. At later stages of your depression, God may seem closer to you in your suffering than ever before. You may have a sense of God's care and consolation.

A guide for prayer is one way to keep yourself—through the chaotic and confusing feelings you experience—attentive to what God is doing in your life.

Some tips

Some days you will want to pray and other days you won't. Some days you may sense God's care, and other days you may be angry with God. Choosing some workable and meaningful prayer forms or rituals will go a long way to keeping you steady through your struggle with depression.

Try the different prayer forms in this book and choose those that seem most helpful to you. Come back to them day after day. The forms you find helpful may shift during the weeks, months, or years you are suffering with depression. Some of the prayers in this book may be meaningful to you at points of your experience of depression, while others may make you angry. You may have to leave them aside. That is okay. Even the feelings with which you react to the prayers are sacred ground. The stability that comes from planning ahead, however, will help you open yourself up to God's healing love.

Pray as you can, not as you can't. But don't give up praying! This wise advice about prayer is especially helpful to remember when you are depressed. Your prayer may be holding on to a holy card of Jesus the Good Shepherd. Your prayer may be sitting quietly and experiencing the stillness of waiting for God. Your prayer may be guided meditation. Your prayer may be a mantra of faith that you repeat during the day. Whatever it is, pray! There is no right or wrong way to pray, because prayer is really about allowing God to work in us. No matter how we do it, as long as we do it, we are on the path of prayer.

These prayers do not promise miracles. Instead, by allowing these prayers to be your companion through your time of depression, you allow God to enter into your sorrow, to share your pain and to raise you to new life.

Before praying—whatever form that takes— you may find it helpful to practice the quieting down and centering preparation on page 3. Depression often makes it difficult to quiet down, to concentrate, to focus. Your mind may race, or you may feel tense and restless. Following a short guide for relaxation can help you to deal with this and make your time of prayer more fruitful.

The most important thing to remember is that you are *worthwhile*. God loves you. God cares about you. God wants to fill you with the precious pearl of his love. God weeps when you weep, and laughs when you laugh. God looks on you with tremendous joy. In your greatest struggles—with grieving, divorce, unemployment, betrayal, mental illness, or anything else that has triggered your depression—God calls you "beautiful," "anointed," "mine."

Preparing for Prayer

"O LORD, your servant is listening."

—*1 Samuel 3:9*

Take everything exactly as it is;
put it in God's hands and leave it to him.
St. Edith Stein

I relax;
I relax the tensions in my body—
in my feet,
in my ankles,
in my knees.
All the tensions
of my body
I let go.

All the distractions
of my mind,
I let go—
the fears,
the hopes,
the anxieties,
the ambitions.
I let them go;
I let all of them go.

I accept myself
just as I am,
with all that I like about myself
and what I wish were different.
I accept myself
just as I am,
at this time.
I feel a powerful light
all around me.
I feel safe in the warmth
of this great light.

I become quiet,
so quiet.
Breathing in
and breathing out,
I let my body settle.
I let my mind settle.
I let myself become still.

4

I feel a profound peace
washing over me,
covering me with a warm blanket
of serenity,
of stillness,
of quiet.

2

Blessings and Affirmations

When we are depressed, what we need to
know is that someone is there for us. "Listen" to these blessings when you feel most
alone. Repeat blessings and affirmations to
yourself as a personal statement of faith.

When you can't hold on to God, God is holding you.
Evelyn Underhill

*J*esus invites you to a very precious intimacy with him in this time of suffering.

—⟡—

*S*ometimes we are unable to feel like we believe God loves us, but don't be afraid—God does!

—⟡—

*Y*ou have Jesus living within you, and Mary as your loving Mother delighting in you as she delights in Jesus. You have your fellow Christians—because we share our faith with one another.

—⟡—

*L*et Jesus believe for you.

*L*et Jesus embrace you.

———❧———

*L*isten for all the ways God tells you, "I love you." This is the deepest reality of your life.

———❧———

*G*od loves you immensely and lives in your heart and he is very pleased with you.

———❧———

*C*hrist's love shines through you. God bless you and keep you safe.

———❧———

3

Seeing More Deeply

Let God walk with you into the broken places of your life that are "holy ground."

The best way to pray is the way you pray best.

Anonymous

The glory of God appears in the dead branches of our lives

A meditation on discouragement (Ex 3:1–6)

In the book of Exodus, God catches Moses' attention in the desert. Moses, a Hebrew who had grown up in Egypt as one of Pharaoh's family, has been exiled after killing an Egyptian he saw striking a Hebrew slave. Here in the desert he has nothing, he is nothing. Everything in him is dead: dreams, ideals, desires. He has only memories of his failure to obtain justice for his fellow Hebrews.

What in you is "dead"? What are the memories that haunt you? From what have you been exiled?

Moses sees a bush that is on fire. The dead branches of the tree, growing in the desert dryness, crackle in the midst of the flames and heat, yet the bush is not consumed by the fire. As Moses approaches to see the tree, God calls out to him, saying, "Moses, Moses, take off your sandals, for the ground on which you are walking is holy ground." Moses takes off his sandals and bows low before the glory of God.

The glory of God appears in the dry branches of your life, in the heat of your depression, a sacred presence that appears as fire, yet does not consume the tree.

Picture yourself as this tree. What does the fire of God feel like as it burns in the dryness of your life? What do you feel toward God as you see your dead branches become the place of God's merciful presence, as the flames dance among the sorrows, not consuming them but respecting, even reverencing them? Can you look on your dead branches with reverence? How does it feel for you to be "holy ground"? Share this with God. ⤺

Those who weep shall be consoled

A prayer of grief and sorrow (Jn 11:1–44)

It has taken Jesus four days to arrive at the home of his dear friend, Lazarus. Though Martha and Mary summoned him immediately after Lazarus took a turn for the worse in his illness, Jesus waited, stating mysteriously that Lazarus' illness was for the glory of God. Now as he approaches the house in which he has spent many wonderful hours with his dear friends, Martha and Mary come to meet him, waves of sorrow almost capsizing their faith. When they really needed Jesus, they felt that he had not been there for them.

Stand beside the two sisters on the road, feeling their sorrow, their struggle to believe in the face of a loss that left them helpless and alone. Do you too carry such sorrow? Have there been times when you felt God has not been there for you?

Jesus' eyes fill with tears as he hears that Lazarus has died. So evident is his sorrow that people begin to notice. "See, Jesus loved Lazarus so much. He too has come to sorrow with us."

Jesus does not abolish our sorrow. Jesus comes to our homes to enter into our sorrow and share its profound pain with us. Jesus mourns, for death ought not to be. He consoles by summoning the dead to life.

Who are the dead for whom you mourn? Can you picture Jesus crying at the tomb of your loved one? Hear Jesus' voice ring out, "Lazarus, come forth! My friend, come forth! Enter now into life for I have conquered death forever!" As your loved one rises and meets Jesus, listen to the words they share with one another. Tell Jesus everything you feel in your heart toward him: gratitude, anger, betrayal.... Share with Jesus your loneliness and grief.

Jesus weeps when he has to admit failure

A song from the ashes of defeat (Lk 13:34)

The wind rustles his garments as Jesus sits down on the hill overlooking Jerusalem. A deep sorrow weighs on his heart. He has made such a long "journey" from the heart of the Trinity to Bethlehem to be Messiah for God's chosen people, to be the One to set God's people free from sin and death. The Son of God has laid aside his divinity and become a baby, a child, a man to live among his people and be their way back to God. *Jerusalem. Jerusalem. How I have longed to be your salvation and your peace. But you would not. Why? How have I failed?*

Find a place near Jesus on the hill overlooking Jerusalem. Can you feel in your heart his sorrow and depression? What have been your Jerusalems? Your failures?

"Jerusalem, Jerusalem. You who have stoned the prophets. How I have longed to gather you as a mother hen gathers her chicks under her wing. But you would not." *Stoned the prophets,* Jesus reflects. A shudder runs through his body. *Stoned the prophets.* An ominous pain begins to grow in the pit of his stomach. "Jerusalem. Jerusalem. Why?"

Watch with reverence as Jesus begins to weep. Consider his sorrow with immense respect and love. Reach out to console him. What does he say to you about your own sorrow? With what reverence does he speak with you about your own failures? Share some time together with the Lord.

All is forgiven

A reflection when feeling guilty or ashamed
(Mt 26:69–76)

Peter hears a cock crow in the distance and he freezes as he remembers his Master's words: "Before the cock crows you will have denied me three times." Deny his Lord. Three times. In an instant the significance of these words begins to tear through his mind. He has denied him, the man he left his former life to follow. The man who has taught him more about God than he thought he would ever understand. The man whom he has confessed to be the Son of the Living God. He has denied this man. In the hour when Jesus needed him most, Peter has claimed not even to know him. A single sob wrenches his heart as he turns and runs into the streets.

Stand beside Peter as he realizes what he has done. He has been so sure that he would be able to give his life for Jesus....What in the world was he thinking: that he could give his life for the Master before the Master lays down his own life for us...? Are there failures in your own life, promises to God never kept, that weigh upon your heart and your conscience? With Peter as your guide, allow them to come to the surface in all their significance for you. ⬎

Stumbling as he goes, Peter runs blindly down the still-dark cobblestoned alley and rounds the corner, only to be cut short by a small procession. He looks up and Jesus, hands bound, looks at him with tired eyes...beautiful eyes that can arrest demons and forgive sinners. Peter is ashamed, but he can't lower his eyes. Jesus holds his gaze as long as he can before he disappears down another street. Peter sinks to the ground and begins to sob.

He knows he has been forgiven. His heart is pierced again with that same look Jesus gave him on the boat three years earlier. "Depart from me, I am a sinful man," Peter confessed. And Jesus' only answer was, "Come and be with me."

If it helps you, pray with a holy card that depicts Jesus looking straight ahead at you with love. Allow your heart to be captured and held by the tenderness of that gaze and the unexpectedness of that love. Confess what in your heart and life gives you most anxiety: memories, hurts, weaknesses, failures, relationships lost.... Picture Jesus putting his hand gently on your head and saying, "I love you. Come and be with me. Come, it is okay. All is forgiven. Come now, and be with me."

Impossible love

Guidance when facing injustice (Lk 23:13–33)

"Whom do you want?" booms out the voice accustomed to deciding the fate of lives. This time he turns the decision over to the public. "Whom do you want?" he says again. "Barabbas? Or this man before you?" Jesus shivers as his gaping wounds are bitten by the early morning air. "Barabbas! Barabbas! Barabbas!" rises the chant. "Then Barabbas it will be," Pilate mumbles under his breath as he motions for a bowl of water to be brought to him. The hearing is over, the decision made. The soldiers grab hold of Jesus and push him forward and out onto the street where he must take up the instrument of his death: the cross.

To what death do you feel handed over? What painful situation is your cross? Who wants to see you fail, or suffer, or give up? Who has been chosen instead of you?

Winding their way through the curious crowds milling through the streets, the procession around Jesus leaves the city and starts on the road that leads to the Place of the Skull, Golgotha. Jesus has handed himself over to his death. He has risked his life by entrusting himself to human beings, who ultimately could not fathom the love he came to be for us. And the world still cannot understand his love, a love that continues to pour itself out to the very end. The miracle of the cross is that Jesus continues to love, to forgive, to seek to understand us, until his last sigh delivers him over to the Father's embrace.

In every situation, even those most tightly controlled by another, there is one thing we can do that is totally our decision: to continue to love the person(s) involved. We may have to remove ourselves from the situation for our own safety and well-being, but we are still free to make the choice to love the person(s) in-

volved, with a love that wants the good, the life, the re-
demption of the other. This is a love that is impossible
for us to have on our own. Share with Jesus the situa-
tion(s) in your life that call for this "impossible love."
Tell Jesus that you are not capable of loving because of
your own pain or hurt. Feel his blood wash you and the
other person(s) involved. Ask Jesus to be the one who
loves with your heart, your gestures, your words. ⌒

Salvation is at work even in our broken dreams

A reflection in times of loss (Jn 19:25–27)

She stands there, watching her Son's life ebb slowly away. She shows strength for his sake, but within she is collapsing with confusion and sorrow. "Your child will be the Son of God. Your son will sit on the throne of David his father forever." Words. Words of an angel, it is true, but now they seem just words. Where is God now? Is this cross David's throne? How can this be happening? Mary doesn't understand, but neither does she need to understand. Even as her every image of God and his love is being shattered against the cross of her Son, she stands in the strength of the logic of faith, which defies analysis and makes sense only from the divine perspective.

Have you, like Mary, stood before an event and watched your life crumble before your eyes? What "children" of your own have you watched die: dreams, promises, relationships? Enter again into the situation, feeling it, hearing it, touching it, absorbing it.

He is stirring above her on the cross raised against the darkening sky. She lifts herself out of her thoughts that he might see her love since she can do nothing more to help him now. The apostle John, who is faithful to the end, reaches out to steady her. "Mother," Jesus says. "Yes, Jesus, I am here. What is it?" "Mother," he says, searching for her face among the bystanders. She steps forward so that he can see her better. "Mother," he says one more time, "take now John to be your son." Her heart breaks. Jesus is really going from her. There is nothing she can do to stop this. Nothing. "John. John, please take care of Mary. Take her as your own mother." Looking up to heaven, then, Jesus says, "It is finished." And his broken body goes limp. He has died.

It seems to Mary she has lost her Son. She is all that is left of the little family that had once lived in Nazareth. The joy she had felt is broken now, a memory that only reminds her of all she has lost. But Jesus has asked her to open her heart to love someone else's son as her own. As the other Marys stand and gather around her, she understands. She is now the mother of all his followers. She is all they have right now to remind them of him.

Have you had to be strong, even as you bore great sorrow in your heart or suffered with depression? Have you watched new dreams and relationships and futures come to birth in the ashes of something you have lost? Gather, as the others beneath the cross, around Mary. Watch and listen. Share with her the burdens you carry. What does she say to you?

4

Moments of Hope

"God is so good and merciful, that to obtain heaven it is sufficient to ask it of him from our hearts."

—*St. Benedict Joseph Labre*

Lord, all things are in your time,
but could we synchronize our watches?

Noel

I believe, Lord, but let me believe more firmly.
I hope, Lord, but let me hope more surely.
I love, Lord, but let me love more warmly.
I repent, Lord, but let me repent more deeply.

St. Anthony Mary Claret

I love the LORD, because he has heard my voice and my supplications. Because he inclined his ear to me, therefore I will call on him as long as I live. The snares of death encompassed me; the pangs of Sheol laid hold on me; I suffered distress and anguish. Then I called on the name of the LORD: "O LORD, I pray, save my life!" Gracious is the LORD, and righteous; our God is merciful. The LORD protects the simple; when I was brought low, he saved me. Return, O my soul, to your rest, for the LORD has dealt bountifully with you.

Psalm 116:1–7

God—who knows what clay he shaped us from and loves us more than a mother can her child—God, who does not lie, has told us that he will not repulse anyone who comes to him.

Venerable Charles de Foucauld

—ᕤ—

My heart was wilderness,
I heard your voice;
my grief divided me,
you held me close;
bitterness consumed me,
you overflowed with trust;
I longed to be with you,
you let me stay.
Janet Morley

*H*ear my prayer, O L ORD; let my cry come to you. Do not hide your face from me in the day of my distress. Incline your ear to me; answer me speedily in the day when I call.

Psalm 102:1–2

*B*ut we have this treasure in clay jars, so that it may be made clear that this extraordinary power belongs to God and does not come from us. We are afflicted in every way, but not crushed; perplexed, but not driven to despair; persecuted, but not forsaken; struck down, but not destroyed; always carrying in the body the death of Jesus, so that the life of Jesus may also be made visible in our bodies.

2 Corinthians 4:7–10a

Show us, good Lord,
the peace we should seek,
the peace we must give,
the peace we can keep,
the peace we must forego,
and the peace you have given
in Jesus Christ our Lord.

Caryl Micklem

———❧———

Rejoice in the Lord always; again I will say, Rejoice. Let your gentleness be known to everyone. The Lord is near. Do not worry about anything, but in everything by prayer and supplication with thanksgiving let your requests be made known to God. And the peace of God, which surpasses all understanding, will guard your hearts and your minds in Christ Jesus.

Philippians 4:4–7

*T*hen I saw a new heaven and a new earth; for the first heaven and the first earth had passed away, and the sea was no more. And I saw the holy city, the new Jerusalem, coming down out of heaven from God, prepared as a bride adorned for her husband. And I heard a loud voice from the throne saying, "See, the home of God is among mortals. He will dwell with them; they will be his peoples, and God himself will be with them; he will wipe every tear from their eyes. Death will be no more; mourning and crying and pain will be no more, for the first things have passed away."

Revelation 21:1–4

———⟶———

*L*ord, look down on me in my infirmities and help me to bear them patiently.

St. Francis of Assisi

More than that, I regard everything as loss because of the surpassing value of knowing Christ Jesus my Lord. For his sake I have suffered the loss of all things, and I regard them as rubbish, in order that I may gain Christ and be found in him.... I want to know Christ and the power of his resurrection and the sharing of his sufferings by becoming like him in his death.

Philippians 3:8–10

O Heart of Love,
I put all my trust in you.
For I fear all things from my own weakness,
but I hope for all things from your goodness.

St. Margaret Mary Alacoque

*S*urrender yourself completely to the care and the everlasting love God has for you. This is your part: you should do this and nothing but this. Leave soul, body, and mind absolutely in his hands.... Act in this way, for I assure you that if you knew the value of your infirmity you would cherish it more than all the good things of earth.

St. Jane de Chantal

———⟨∽⟩———

*I*ncline your ear, O LORD, and answer me, for I am poor and needy. Preserve my life, for I am devoted to you; save your servant who trusts in you. You are my God; be gracious to me, O LORD, for to you do I cry all day long. Gladden the soul of your servant, for to you, O LORD, I lift up my soul.

Psalm 86:1–4

*A*las, my only true love has vanished,
From his favor I am banished.
Gone that smile which flashed so bright.
Gone my heart's once radiant light.
How could he leave me?
Did his promise deceive me?
Ah no! He will return.
Soon, soon my heart will burn!
Come you, my pleasure,
And I shall love you without measure.

St. Rose of Lima

*C*ast yourself into the arms of God
and be very sure that if he wants anything of
     you,
he will fit you for the work
and give you strength.

St. Philip Neri

*W*hatever did not fit in with my plan
did lie within the plan of God.
I have an ever deeper and firmer belief
that nothing is merely an accident
when seen in the light of God,
that my whole life
down to the smallest details
has been marked out for me
in the plan of Divine Providence
and has a completely coherent meaning
in God's all-seeing eyes.
And so I am beginning to rejoice
in the light of glory
wherein this meaning
will be unveiled to me.

St. Edith Stein

*L*et nothing disturb you,
nothing frighten you,
all things are passing.
Patient endurance
attains all things:
one who God possesses
wants nothing,
for God alone suffices.

St. Teresa of Avila

5

Praying Through Depression

"I feel alone and locked in darkness."

—*Donna Jean*

Sometimes our light goes out,
but it is blown into flame by another.
Albert Schweitzer

Shine brightly and warm the frozen ground of my soul. Help me to face my fears, my losses, my pain. I have done what I could to reach out for help and you have given me such support through others. Hold me up by their care so that when the fear of losing myself overwhelms me, I am not alone. Take me to your Heart, Sweet Jesus. Mary, lead me and hold me. As one friend told me, "I believe that Providence rises before the dawn."

Marie

O God,
my world seems to be crumbling.
Everything is caving in on me.
I feel alone and locked in darkness.

O God,
I don't even feel like praying.
But I know I need you
now more than ever.

O God,
are you really with me?
Are you holding me in the palm of your hand?
Are you providing for me like the lilies of the
    field?

I don't feel your presence.
I don't even feel lovable.

Please accept me in this sorry state.
Hear my poor prayer.

Wash away this darkness,
and send me a glimmer of comfort.
Give me the life that you promise,
O God.

Donna Jean

———❧———

*J*esus, I trust in your grace, that you love me, and that you are guarding me with your grace. I want to rest in your peace. I trust in those persons you have sent in my life to help me. I trust in you.

Anne

When my life was turned upside down by an unforeseen separation and divorce, I created this litany to affirm the things I wanted to be. It is easy to personalize.

Lord, all things are possible with your grace.
By the grace of God...
I am healthy: mentally, spiritually and physically.
By the grace of God...
I have faith not fear.
By the grace of God...
I am strong, resilient, and confident.
By the grace of God...
I am a good wife, mother, daughter, sister,
     friend, neighbor, and co-worker.
By the grace of God...
I am calm inside and out.
By the grace of God...
I am resourceful, intuitive, and creative.

By the grace of God...

I am energetic, mentally and physically.

By the grace of God...

I have the right balance, perspective, and
priorities in my life.

By the grace of God...

I have good judgment and make smart
decisions.

By the grace of God...

I have a positive mental attitude.

By the grace of God...

I am completely healed and whole.

By the grace of God...

I am filled with 57 years of blessings.

By the grace of God...

I put my life in your hands. Amen

Noel

The Trinity is our maker. The Trinity is our keeper.
The Trinity is our everlasting lover.
The Trinity is our endless joy.

Blessed Julian of Norwich

I am surrounded and filled with darkness, my God. It seems to cling to me. I walk around but see and understand nothing. Where are you, my Light? You said, "I am the Light." You healed the man born blind. What you did for others, do now for me. Have pity on *me*. Shed your light into my mind, into my heart. Please be the Sun of my life. Even if this night of my life does not become day at this time, let a ray of your Sun penetrate the darkness—even a little—and warm my heart.

Patrick

I wish I could feel something, anything.
But I feel nothing. I feel dead inside.
So I put on a smile. It's so hard to smile.
It takes all the energy I have (and I don't have
    much)
to smile at school, in front of my friends,
so nobody knows.
And then I collapse when I get home—all I
    want to do is sleep.
They open my door—Are you okay?
LEAVE ME ALONE!
No, don't go, please...but just listen to me.
God, help my parents to listen to me
without judging,
without trying to make it better,
without saying it will pass,
without trying to fix it,
without talking about themselves,
without words.

Just let them hold me and show me that God
    loves me.
God thinks I'm precious and wonderful.
God thinks I'm worth saving.
He will wait for my smile, however long it takes,
and in the meantime, he will smile for me.

Anonymous teenager

———— ❧ ————

Lord,
in the darkness you are there, waiting for me
    in the silence of my heart.
You alone comfort me and give me hope.
You guide me, walking hand in hand with me.
Fill my heart with love for you.
I want to live through this depression with all
    the love that you desire of me. Amen.

Rita

*I*n a time before the darkness,
a time before the storm
I knew you.
Your gaze was a familiar touch to me,
and I knew the sounds of laughter.
But now it's only mocking I hear and I feel not
the touch of the wind
and you've been gone so long.
How silent is the darkness.

It seems my mind retreats at the sound of
    your name
and thoughts of you are jumbled in the trivia
    of the day.
It seems my mind no longer holds an image
    of your face,
or can no longer respond to the simple touch
    of your grace.
I stand at the edge of your minions

a shadow without a face
in an arena where the light refuses to leave a
  sparkle or a trace.
What is this lonely darkness
that wraps me like a cloak?
That steals away forever your warmth and the
  love that it evokes?
Cursed be the harrowing night
that separates one from one, and in my mind
  I wonder:
Will I ever see the Sun?

Sister Thomas

Spinning in my own head,
racing are my thoughts;
splitting is what it feels like for my brain.
My moods are on a roller coaster ride.
The ride never ends, and suddenly one sunny
    day began.
What is happening to me?
Why do I feel so out of control?
What is left in life for me to go through this
    on a daily basis?
The pain sometimes is unbearable.
It is the same pain that Christ suffered for me
    and because of this I must choose to live
    even if nothing makes sense most of the
    time.

    Ruth

O Lord, in your mercy, please listen to my
    crying for you.
My mind is confused and in distress.
I am in fear of losing the knowledge of your
    Truth.
In your compassion, my Lord, you emptied
    my mind of all knowledge.
I pray for you to enlighten my mind,
but instead you guide my heart.
For it is in my heart that you dwell.
There is where I find your love.
For if I lose all knowledge, above all, my
    Lord, it is your love
that will always belong to me.
And, in truth, O Lord, I will always love you.
Amen.

Marlene

I consider that the sufferings of this present time
are not worth comparing with the glory
about to be revealed to us.

Romans 8:18–19

O Lord, this day has been so difficult. Wave after wave of dark thoughts, sadness, and self-recriminations beating down upon me like a storm at sea that will not end.

And now night.

Exhausted and spent from battling the waves, my bones feel too heavy for my muscles to move—but I cannot sleep.

Yet, I will trust your word, Lord. I will hold on to your promise, if only with a feeble grip. I will not be destroyed. I will not be overwhelmed. You made the sandy shore, the sea's limit, which by eternal decree it may not overstep. Toss though it may it is to no avail; though its billows roar, they cannot pass. I am safe. I can rest *(based on Jeremiah 5:22)*.

Mary

Colon cancer, operation, chemotherapy...
The words all ran together.
That can't be me the doctor is talking about.
    God help me, it can't be me.

Husband, father, grandfather...
I've got to stay strong for my family. Thank
    God for my family.
They are my strength.

The operation is over, the chemo has started,
my hair has fallen out,
my nails are cracking and splitting.
I find it hard to walk when the soles of my
    feet hurt so much.

I look in the mirror
and don't recognize the man I see there.
God, give me the courage to endure this,
and with your help to survive it.

I try to hide behind a smile and a joke,
But inside I am afraid.
I can't let it show because
I am the husband, the father, the grandfather.

I want to watch many more baseball games,
hockey games and football games
with my son, daughters, and grandchildren.
I still have more things to tell them...more
    stories to share.

Is it my time, God? I hope not.
  Bob

God, it seems like I was better off being in total depression rather than feeling all the pain. I need to be loved completely. There is a feeling of loss, of emptiness and yearning along with anger at having to suffer this! It's not fair being mentally ill and needing *so* much. Suffering is unfair. God, why do you let it be? Why did you suffer so horrendously? What does salvation mean? Suffer, then go to heaven? *I am angry!* No one can take away my right to be angry anymore. God, how can you stand to be part of this world? How can you choose to abide in us and in all things?

The paradox of your presence and care melts away the anger. All will be well in the end. This day is new—full of emotion and fears, but, God, you embrace me in the pain, inside and out. I need, yet I have all I need for now. You never leave me alone. You send your "angels" to comfort me through friends and professional help. My cynical side wants to say it's all a fairy tale to make us feel better temporarily. But, the truth is far more real than my doubts and fears. Within every fiber of my being, God, you are. The warmth flows through me like blood in the body—in the Body of Christ. Oh, let it flow through me to warm my cold, angry soul today.

Michael

*P*lease help me, Lord, as I pray to live again
    another day.
I sit here and look about and ponder my fate.
Help me, O Lord, to overcome my days of
    anxiety and depression.
I have so much to be thankful for: my mate,
    my loving, supportive family,
    and a host of friends.
But most of all, Lord, I have you to turn to
    in my hours of need.
During these many months of cancer
    treatments,
the physical pain and mental anguish,
I have come to know that birth and death are
    but one,
neither the coming or going is of any conse-
    quence.
What is of consequence is the beauty that one
    gathers in this interlude of life...

life is a circle...a gift from God.
True happiness could never be complete if we
   never have watched with sorrow.
So, I look to the stars.
Life is more radiant by the darkness of
   despair.
No, not despair. We leave our footprints in the
   sand.
Believe! Keep Faith! Trust in the Lord!
   Grace...mercy...peace.

Nancy

I feel you gently tugging the strings of my
   heart,
drawing me closer to your light,
to your healing touch.

Thomas

*J*esus, thank you for the grace to feel better today! Guard my mind, my heart, my feelings. Help me to reach out to others. Help me also to accept my illness once again. It's easy to do this right now, but it's quite another thing when I am in pain. Give me the grace to embrace my cross with courage. When I start worrying about the future with my obsessive thoughts, be there with me in the present moment. I cannot do this on my own, Lord. Place me in your open, wounded heart, and keep me safe when all in me and around me is in turmoil. Thank you for the peace of this day. Amen.

Janelle

Out of the depths of my despair I call to you, Lord—Lord, hear me.

It has been six months and I still can't find a job. I am very worried since my family is dependent on my income. If nothing comes through, I will lose my home and my savings.

I look to you for mercy; I look to you for help—a help that will surely come.

What have I to do but wait for your help? Like a watchman set on a tower waiting for daybreak I will wait.

Has the daybreak ever failed to come? Has the sun ever failed to rise in its time? *(based on Psalm 130)*

Montgomery

My days are like an eternity. It sounds crazy, but I feel almost like I deserve to suffer depression. Why? I don't know the answer. I know God does not want me to. But I feel guilty and so discouraged. I gave so much to other people when they needed me, and now.... No one remembers. No one stops in to see how I am doing. No one cares.

Sometimes I wish I had never been born. God forgive me for saying that, but it is just that it is so painful going on day after day.

Pauline

*L*ord, today I envisioned my dying mother's face in her last agony. I see your face in hers, your eyes in hers. Your perspiration was hers. Your struggle to breathe was hers. Yet, she silently lay there in her agony waiting, accepting as you did, Lord. I know now as I ponder that she gave herself totally to you because she said to me, "I need to let go," and she did, and in her suffering, she said, "God is so good to me." When she died she blew her last breath toward me as if to say, "Live on, honey." I know, Lord, that you are as close to me as a breath, and even closer, you are in my heart.

Laura Rosemarie

I believe, God,
though I cannot see
or hear or feel your presence.
I believe and I trust.

You are the very life within me:
my breath, my heartbeat.
You are within, near me in my pain and my
     emptiness,
my void.

I believe.

Open my heart to gratitude
so that my pain and my emptiness
may be fruitful,
that my darkness may be a creative space
where I come to know you in a new way,
deep and intimate,
deeper and more real than words or images.

And with an open heart
may your stillness and peace and faithfulness
pour out of my being to others.

In the name of Jesus.
Amen.

Maire nic Dhia

———

I am so afraid that you will leave me, my God. Others abandoned me; I feel very scared. Teach me, show me you are with me today and will be with me for all the tomorrows.

Pattie

*J*esus, the doctor just called. At my last check-up when I saw that my blood counts had dropped, that sinking feeling hit me. When I had to go for a bone marrow biopsy, I knew what it meant. Still, I was hoping. After the test I had to wait a while for the results. Every time the phone rang my stomach did a flip-flop. But now at least I know the truth: the results show that the "hairy cells" have infiltrated the bone marrow again. "Hairy-cell leukemia"—it's been almost five years since I first got it and I had been hoping that I could make it past that five-year mark. I don't understand why it returned. I did everything I could to make it stay in remission; I did all the "right" things: exercise, good nutrition, vitamins....

Now I still feel like I'm in a state of shock. I must be in denial, because I can't really believe what's happening. I'm just numb. So I'll do what

I always do: try to control it with knowledge. Have patience with me as I look up all my favorite health sites on the internet in the hope that they can offer me some "magic" cure. I know they really can't, but I have to try.

Lord, eventually I'll learn, but not now, not just yet. Teach me that you are in control of my life, not me. Teach me to remember that I can't control my health. Help me to let go of my burning desire to do it all myself. You are always with me, but I often forget that. When I go to the hospital for a week of chemotherapy, you'll be there. When my arm starts to hurt from having a needle stuck in it for so long, you'll be there. When I can't sleep because of all the noise in the hospital, you'll be there. When my friends come to visit me, you'll be there with them. Thank you for their help and support! Most of all, when the treatment is over and I get well again—because I know you still have work for me to do here—help me to spend what remains of my life in bringing your love to others.

Marianne

When I look into the mirror, who do I see?
A man maturing at age thirty-three.
Boozing and drugging, out of control,
confined yet again. How'd I get in this hole?

Coke and booze promised me bliss in the end,
deceived me by saying, "I'm your best friend."
But one friend doesn't turn another into a
    slave
or shovel dirt on another friend's grave.

Addiction takes everything; nothing is saved.
With prison and death this highway is paved.
Because of drug abuse this route was my destiny
'til gratitude caused me to look into a mirror
    at age thirty-three.

Peter

*F*or a long time now I have believed that I am a bad person, my Friend. This belief has darkened my life and destroyed my joy. I have suffered terribly because I believed those who told me by their words or behavior, "You are bad." They were wrong! You created me good. Help me to believe this truth! You came to save. Save me, my trustworthy God. Loosen the bonds of old beliefs and old memories that still hold me captive.

Langley

6

When You Can't Pray

Help me, Lord, one minute at a time.

*Surrender yourself completely to the care
and the everlasting love God has for you.*

St. Jane de Chantal

Breath Prayers

I breathe in Light, and breathe out sorrow.

—❧—

*J*esus is with me.

—❧—

*G*od, give me joy again.

—❧—

*G*od, come to my assistance.
O Lord, make haste to help me.

—❧—

*J*esus, Son of God, have mercy on me.

———❧———

*D*o not be afraid, you are mine.

———❧———

*L*ord, you are greater than all my sorrow.

———❧———

*J*esus, I trust in you.

———❧———

I'm tired of the pain and I want to be healed. I want to be healed.

———❧———

78

Make me unafraid of love.

—⁓—

Lord, you are close to the brokenhearted.

—⁓—

Lord, accomplish in me yourself everything that you desire of me.

—⁓—

Rituals

Keep a favorite picture of Jesus close to you where you can see it often.

—⁓—

*H*old on to a holy card during the long nights when you can't sleep.

———❧———

*H*old a rosary in your hands.

———❧———

*W*hen you are walking say to God: With every step I renew my trust.

———❧———

*S*it in the sun and absorb the light and the warmth. Imagine yourself being surrounded and permeated with God's love.

———❧———

*W*ear a medal of Jesus or Mary.

———ے———

*K*eep holy water in your house and use it for a simple blessing.

———ے———

*L*isten to Christian music to lift your spirits.

———ے———

7

From Those Who've Been There

"Lord, WHERE WERE YOU?"

—*Annie*

Go forth without fear, for he who created you
has made you holy, has always protected you,
and loves you as a mother.

St. Clare of Assisi

Lord, you reveal to me my inner beauty and heal me of the lies I tell myself, lies that keep me from experiencing my full reality. I have always lived feeling "less" than others, excluded or not good enough. Shame is at the root of my self-understanding—a feeling so deep that I cannot get a hold of it, contain it and toss it out. I am swimming in this insecurity.

Yet what a relief to admit it to you and to another, to accept it, to live despite it. My determination to enjoy life and others, to treat myself with the respect that has always been due to me, and to treat others with equal respect springs from this inner pain and loss. I offer my pain in union with the abandoned Crucified One so that peace may enter my being, and through me to another part of your Body. Amen.

Jeanne

On those horrible nights when you can do nothing but lie in bed and ruminate, try to imagine a wooden box with a lid, any wooden box you can imagine: large or small, fancy or plain. Watch each negative thought—every adjective, noun, and image—travel from your head into the box. Watch all those things you tell yourself: "useless," "hopeless," "broken," float from your head and into the wooden box. See the scenes from your life that wound you over and over wash out of your head and into the box.

Then say the following verse as many times as you want until you are ready to "close" the box: "For my power is made perfect in weakness" (2 Cor 12:9).

Now imagine Jesus standing before you. We all have our own special image of him and our reaction to his presence. For me, he lifts my bowed head and smiles at me, much like a father does with a child who is feeling ashamed or has been hurt. When he departs, open the box.

Watch each positive thought come out of the box and surround you like clouds or perhaps a warm blanket. Imagine all the positive images and adjectives you "wish" or "want" to be: energetic, playful, hardworking, needed, loved, healed. See the positive scenes of how you want to "BE" in your life. Linger in the mental imagery of these positive thoughts as long as you want. (I usually fall asleep, finally, in this positive comfort zone.)

Remembering that the Lord can take all the faults, all the bad, and transform them into good can keep hope alive for one more night.

Jennifer

*F*ather, most holy One, I thank you for all those times when you were with me in my moments of darkness, of weakness, or of suffering. Your love seemed to be above me, below me, before me, behind me, all around me, embracing me, holding me, supporting me, healing me. I remember with gratitude the encouragement of friends and the many people who have cared about me. May this memory of your goodness fill my every coming day with hope. I trust you. Amen.

James

———ॐ———

*O*nce when my obsessive thoughts were overwhelming I asked Jesus to help me. I heard in my heart, "You are participating in my passion." I believe that each of us participates in Jesus' passion in some manner. For some of us maybe it is through physical pain. For others it might be sor-

row and loss. For still others it may be the foolish-
ness and humiliation of Jesus' crucifixion. But for
me, I believe it is the crowning of thorns that is the
mystery of Jesus' passion that I live most often.

Blake

*D*ear God, thank you for my mood disorder.
Thank you for the challenges and suffering it
brings me. Thank you for choosing me to understand the cross more. Help me to never lose sight
of your love. Help me to always call on you when I
feel like I can't handle my mood disorder anymore. Bring the right doctors, medications, and
therapists into my life. Let me live every day, hour,
minute, and second like it was my last. Also, let me
be your instrument of compassion for the world.

I ask this all in Jesus' name. Amen.

Ruth

*D*ear Lord,
At times like these it can be hard
just to get through another day,
but I choose to trust in you
and not to give in to all my fears.
I can't figure out the future,
but I can make it through today.
I want to rejoice that you have given me
    another day.
I want to thank you for all that you have given
    me already...
and for the blessings that you will give me
    today....
I know that your grace will be enough for me
    this day,
for your "power shows up best in weak
    people" (2 Cor 12:9).

St. Paul goes on to say:

"Now I am glad to boast about how weak I
     am;

I am glad to be a living demonstration of
     Christ's power,

instead of showing off my own power and
     abilities...

for when I am weak, then I am strong—

the less I have, the more I depend on him"
     (2 Cor 12:9–10, *The Living Bible*).

Show me the path that I must walk today.

Grant me the grace to live today in peace and
     serenity.

Thank you for another day.

I choose to live this day.

I choose you, O Lord.

   Elizabeth

My real "holy hours" are those hours when sufferings of body and soul come to overwhelm me. Those hours when God hands me the chalice of suffering...

Karl Rahner

*T*hank you, Lord, for being with me in what I thought were the darkest days of my life, the days following my miscarriage. Thank you for showing me how Abraham was willing to surrender his son Isaac's future to your perfect will. It was with that example that I was able to trust you to know what was better for my life and to be able to give my child back to you. And with the broken heart of my dreams you blessed me with such sweet peace that I can now testify of your love to the many hearts that will also hurt in this way. Thank you, Lord, for seeing the big picture and making it possible for my heart to always be willing to say, "I surrender all."

Mary

I feel like you are bending down to me, Lord, in my brokenness, in my sense of being unlovable. It's like being turned around 180 degrees by challenging me to love above all things. You are in fact assuming that I have been loved *first* by you, who alone can enable me to love. My experience of human love has been far from unconditional, but I have been given a glimpse of your infinite love through special people in my life today. I can't remain in the past and allow my wounds to fester. As I reach out for others' help and accept care from others, I am learning how to love myself in order that I may enjoy your love. "God loved me, and gave his life for me." What power there is in your love.

Phoebe

Lord, my mind is racing and I feel so anxious. Help me to trust! I want to trust! You are holding me in your powerful and protective hands. You love me. You know my anguish. I believe you are with me and I believe you will provide for me. I offer this pain in union with the anguish you suffered in Gethsemane. I especially make this offering with you in Mass and Communion, and pray for my brothers and sisters who are anxious and worried but do not have the help of others or medication, those alone and without any hope. Let them experience your tenderness; embrace them and let them know you are with them. Amen.

Luam

Within the confines of my heart certain
   darkness exists.
And how accustomed I've become
to Living with the Night!
Anger...hostility...rage...self-hate...rash
   judgments
seem to prevail at times to my utter dismay.
And now you say embrace them....
Soften them with Love....
The fear...disgust...contingency,
need the healing Light.
To embrace those feelings
I've been dodging for years....at an unknown
   cost...the price of terror?
Another's strength is needed.
I've proved too weak before.
Let your Light be mine in the squalid
   darkness.

Teach me gentleness of mind and heart.
Open me to your embrace and the warmth of
   your Love.

   José

———⌒∾———

My God, how long can I go on like this? My own life is drained from me. I would like to die, but death won't come to bring me relief. I am angry, depressed, and grieving for what I've done. Resentment, guilt, shame never seem to leave my soul. If I think about my child, I say, "O God, I am so sorry." It's the only prayer I know. I *grieve* for the loss of the child I'll never hold. But you reveal yourself as Provider, Protector and Savior. In your love and forgiveness wash my shame away. You enfold me in your arms as *your* child, and in this embrace of yours I will find my child again. Amen.

   Elaine

I am 56 years old this year, a mother and grandmother, and have had some time to see the workings of God. It has been my "experience" to observe that there is a tailor-made test for every juncture of life, and if it doesn't feel as if this time all really is lost—this time I really am going to die—then it is not a useful test. And there is no pass or fail. Just surrender. Just letting go more and more until you don't realize that you have lost your grip.... Life is a continual lesson in learning that God doesn't take away our problems, but comes to be with us in them, using them to transform us into the people we really want to become, changing our focus from the illusory demands of the material world to the sure certainty of life in the Spirit.

Mary

8

Stations of the Cross

By Kathryn James Hermes, FSP

By your holy cross you have redeemed the world.

The most beautiful Credo is the one
we pronounce in our hour of darkness.

Padre Pio

*T*he Stations of the Cross are a powerful way of entering into the mystery of Jesus' gift of himself to us. As can be seen in the earliest writings of the Christians, some of which are found in the Bible, it is clear that the followers of Jesus told and retold the story of his passion, death, and resurrection. Through the first fourteen centuries after Jesus' life and death, pilgrims traveled to Jerusalem in order to see the places where Jesus had suffered and died. In the 1500's, when travel was not easy, villages all over Europe created replicas of the "way of the cross," and eventually these became the set of fifteen stations we now find in almost every Catholic church in the world. While most churches have the same set of stations, various other stations remember different events along the *Via Crucis*. I have chosen fourteen events on the way of the cross in which Jesus models for me how to be in right relationship with God, myself, and others. When I find myself upset or troubled I pray these stations and allow Jesus to heal the distortions in my thinking and teach me how to love in truth. May they be for you, as they have been for me, a path to peace and serenity.

✜ FIRST STATION ✜

Jesus in the Garden of Gethsemane

Jesus, when situations seem to be completely successful or devastating failures, help me to find the mystery of the "in-between" where failures are successes, and some successes are partly failures. Through what seemed your failure on the cross, we were all redeemed and have gained eternal life. Jesus, in my moments of agony, may I feel you near to me as a comfort and guide.

✛ SECOND STATION ✛

Jesus, Betrayed by Judas, Is Arrested

Jesus, when I feel let down by people I have trusted, or don't understand what someone's words or actions mean, give me the courage to ask for clarifications and explanations, instead of coming to conclusions based on just one event. As you maintained your respect for Judas till the end, teach me to respect the mystery of the other person whom I feel has hurt me. Jesus, when my moods start plummeting because of something another says or does, hold me in your arms.

✛ THIRD STATION ✛

Jesus Is Condemned by the Sanhedrin

Jesus, help me keep the big things big, but help me especially to keep all the little things in my life *little*. When everything seems to be turning into a catastrophe, I want to remember you as you stood before the Sanhedrin with self-respect, trusting that your Father would take care of you. Jesus, when the world seems like it is spinning out of control, remind me of *our* Father's care.

✝ FOURTH STATION ✝

Jesus Is Denied by Peter

Jesus, help me to realize that there are things that are out of my control, that no matter how hard I try, I cannot make everything perfect. Help me to enter into the mystery of powerlessness, when your hand-picked apostle denied he even knew you, and left you to suffer alone. Did you wonder why you had worked so hard to teach this man, who in the end denied you? Or did you hand the future of your kingdom over to God, since your death meant the giving up of all control? Jesus, when I think I am in control, gently pry open my hands and help me let go. Teach me to laugh and play again.

✚ FIFTH STATION ✚

Jesus Is Judged by Pilate

Jesus, stand beside me when I feel like others are judging me or putting me down. Did you feel embarrassed when you were condemned in front of all those people? I feel like that sometimes. I interpret people's comments, or even the way they look at me, as a condemnation or ridicule. Jesus, when I feel like everyone is looking at me, hide me in the shelter of your love.

✝ SIXTH STATION ✝

Jesus Is Scourged and Crowned with Thorns

Jesus, your scourging and crowning with thorns were so unfair. What were you thinking while the soldiers scourged you and then made fun of you, crowning you with thorns and mocking you as a king? I'd be angry with them for making a fool of me. But you saw the larger picture. You knew life isn't all about fairness, that sometimes we will be treated unjustly. Jesus, when I don't think that others are treating me fairly, help me to remember that you weren't treated fairly, that you have walked this road ahead of me, that in the mystery of suffering I can unite my suffering to yours and share in the work of salvation with you.

✝ SEVENTH STATION ✝

Jesus Bears the Cross

Jesus, when you started out through the crowded streets of Jerusalem toward Calvary, how did you feel about yourself? After all that had happened to you, were you wondering if maybe you had been wrong? Perhaps if you had done things a different way, you wouldn't have ended up a man condemned to die as a criminal? Were you afraid as the people bustled around you, trying to stay clear of the soldiers? Sometimes I feel pretty bad about myself. I carry my cross of depression and I think I'm no good, a failure, ugly. Jesus, when I feel this way about myself, help me to remember that it isn't true. Help me to carry my cross beside you, to look into your eyes, and there to see who I truly am, there, in your eyes which always look on me with love.

✝ EIGHTH STATION ✝

Jesus Is Helped by Simon the Cyrenian to Carry the Cross

Jesus, did you hope that someone would help you carry the cross, or were you surprised that Simon was told to take your cross on his shoulders? Many times I expect or demand a Simon to appear, someone to change their attitude and help me out a little. When my Simon doesn't appear, Lord, you be my Simon, and don't let me become bitter and blame everyone else for my problems. Jesus, let me see your face, and I shall be saved.

✝ NINTH STATION ✝

Jesus Meets the Women of Jerusalem

Jesus, these women of Jerusalem were so compassionate. What did they see in you? It would have been so easy for you to curse the whole human race for the way you were being treated. But you didn't fall into the trap of labeling everyone because of some people's actions. You were still open to accept the kindnesses these women showed you. When I make broad judgments because of the actions of a few, send me someone like these women to remind me of the beauty of life and the ultimate reliability of love.

✛ TENTH STATION ✛

Jesus Is Crucified

If you wanted to, Jesus, you could have had the last word. You could have justified yourself, proven to everyone around your cross that you had been right all along and that you really were God's Son. "Come down off your cross and we'll believe," the onlookers taunted. You could have done what they asked. Jesus, it is so hard not to have the last word, not to always be right...especially when I *am* right. Jesus, Truth, may I trust that the truth will always come out in the end, that it is not justifying myself with others that matters. It is being in a right relationship with you, myself, and others that ultimately counts.

✛ ELEVENTH STATION ✛

Jesus Promises His Kingdom to the Good Thief

The good thief had a lot of nerve to trust you in those last moments before his death. You could have told him that he should never have broken the law in the first place, but you didn't. You saw that life is about more than rules, though they have their place. Life is about reconciliation and acceptance, a love that creates goodness around itself. When I make "should" statements to myself or others, teach me the mystery of creative love that can promise eternal happiness to repentant criminals.

✝ TWELFTH STATION ✝

Jesus Speaks to His Mother and the Disciple

It must have been hard for Mary to stand beneath your cross. She was surrounded by people who wanted to see you dead. She saw the child she had cradled in her arms stretched beyond recognition on the arms of the cross. She heard you promising the good thief eternal happiness in your kingdom. She received the charge of caring for John as a son. Truly, beneath the cross all of us became her children. Mary was able to hold the beauty and the pain of those last hours of your life together, neither lashing out in anger nor discounting the good. Jesus, entrust me again to such a wonderful Mother, that I might neither discount the good in and around me, nor magnify the bad. Mary, be my sure hope.

✠ THIRTEENTH STATION ✠

Jesus Dies on the Cross

Jesus, no one knew your final thoughts as you died. There are the traditional "seven last words" recorded in the Gospels, but I wonder what else you were thinking. Did you think of me? Sometimes I think I'm a mind reader and am often suspicious of other people's attitudes toward me. I never have to be afraid of what you think of me, however, because you can only love. You create love all around you. Jesus, help me believe in your love.

✟ FOURTEENTH STATION ✟

Jesus Is Placed in the Tomb

I can imagine all of nature in mourning when you, my Jesus, were placed in the tomb, as if all living things cradled your sacred, lifeless body. Jesus, I am never alone. I am cradled in your Father's arms, held by the universe, connected by the web of life to the history of every other human person who has ever lived on this planet. And now I can feel how all creation groans and waits for *my* resurrection, for the moment of exaltation when tears will be wiped away and sorrow will be no more. Jesus, resurrected Lord and Savior, be my salvation. Amen.

9

The Seven Sorrows of Mary

By Sharon Anne Legere, FSP

"Is any sorrow like the sorrow that afflicts me?"

—*Lamentations 1:12*

The human being is always unique and unrepeatable;
somebody thought of and chosen from eternity.

John Paul II

*T*he devotion to the Seven Sorrows of Mary has its origin in the Gospels: Simeon's prophecy that a sword would pierce Mary's heart and that she would stand beneath the cross.

The celebration and veneration of Mary's sorrows and compassion go back to the fourth or fifth century. The devotion became particularly widespread with the Franciscans in the thirteenth century, and became the principal devotion of the Servites in 1233. The liturgical feast of Our Lady of Sorrows is September 15. Spanish-speaking countries honor the Virgin of Solitude (or *Virgen de la Soledad)* on Holy Saturday (the day before Easter).

It is hard to express all the confidence I have in Mary's compassion, love, and protection. When my moods become dark, I have come more and more to turn to Mary to calm me and inspire me with hope. She suffered in her life in so many ways. Meditating on her sorrows helps me to have patience and serenity in coping with my own sorrows and pain. As one who knew intense sorrow beneath the cross, Mary gently comforts all who are afflicted.

Entrusting Oneself to Mary

Receive me, O Mary, my Mother, Teacher, and Queen, among those whom you love, nourish, sanctify, and guide. I place myself entirely into your hands. Lead me to Jesus. Obtain for me the grace to know, imitate, and love him evermore. Enlighten me, strengthen me, sanctify me. Amen.

THE FIRST SORROW

The Prophecy of Simeon

Lk 2:22–35

Then Simeon blessed them and said to his mother Mary, "This child is destined for the falling and the rising of many in Israel, and to be a sign that will be opposed so that the inner thoughts of many will be revealed— and a sword will pierce your own soul too" (Lk 2:34).

Mary, *strength* for those who struggle with depression, what went through your mind as you heard these words about you and your Son's future? I, too, have heard words such as these: "You are depressed." "You need hospitalization." "We need to try a new medication." "You should start therapy." When I hear the "prophecy" of what seems to be only sorrow ahead of me, give me the

119

courage with which you faced your life, with no illusions about the pain that awaited you somewhere, somehow, someday in the future. You knew that the Father held you in his hand. Mary, strength of the struggling, pray for me that I might walk with courage into the night.

THE SECOND SORROW

The Flight into Egypt

Mt 2:13–21

Now after they had left, an angel of the Lord appeared to Joseph in a dream and said, "Get up, take the child and his mother, and flee to Egypt, and remain there until I tell you; for Herod is about to search for the child, to destroy him" (Mt 2:13).

Mary, model of *patience*, the years that passed in Egypt must have been painfully slow. They were years of exile for you. You and your family were refugees. I feel "exiled" from life, the life others lead—the life of laughter and fun, joy and consolation. I am a refugee, living isolated in a no-man's-land, here where very few understand what I feel. Pray for me that I may live with your patience, trusting in the slow process at work in the darkness that shrouds my life. Mary, patience of the waiting, I place my trust in you.

THE THIRD SORROW

The Loss of Jesus in the Temple

Lk 2:41–50

His mother said to him, "Child, why have you treated us like this? Look, your father and I have been searching for you in great anxiety" (Lk 2:48).

Mary, my *refuge,* I think I know what you might have felt as you searched frantically for your Son in

Jerusalem: Have I failed the Father in caring for his Son? What is going to happen if I can't find him? And when you did find Jesus in the temple, he didn't really offer you an explanation, but left you even more puzzled. Pray for me when I feel a deep sense of guilt because God seems so far away, because I can't seem to pray, or because I fear that God gave this depression to me as a punishment. Mary, refuge of sinners, save me from my fears.

THE FOURTH SORROW

Mary Meets Jesus Carrying the Cross

Jn 19:1; Lk 23:26–32

As they led him away, they seized a man, Simon of Cyrene, who was coming from the country, and they laid the cross on him, and made him carry it behind Jesus. A great number of the people followed him (Lk 23:26–27).

Mary, my *support,* how could you bear this public humiliation of your Son and yourself? You were there with your Son, wherever he looked, giving him support and courage. I often feel distrustful of people around me. I feel like others are watching me, that my depression is public knowledge, that everybody knows and sees the struggle, that somehow I am less a person. Surround me with your presence when I feel the curious stares. Mary, support of the struggling, walk by my side and let me walk in your courage.

THE FIFTH SORROW

Mary Stands Beneath the Cross

*Mk 15:22; Jn 19:18, 25–27; Mk 15:34;
Lk 23:46*

Standing near the cross of Jesus were his mother, and his mother's sister, Mary the wife of Clopas, and Mary Magdalene. When Jesus saw his mother and the disciple whom he loved standing beside her, he said to his mother, "Woman, here is your son" (Jn 19:25–26).

Mary, my *comfort,* standing beneath the cross you grasped for any glimpse of hope as you watched and waited and loved—loved until the last breath of your Son. The joy of your motherhood was dead. In that moment your faith may have been strong, but did your heart question, "Why? What is the meaning of all this?" When I feel alone and abandoned by God, when my last dreams die and all I can come up with is questions, the mysteries of your sorrowful heart give me hope. Mary, comfort of the suffering, comfort me.

THE SIXTH SORROW

Mary Receives the Dead Body of Jesus

Jn 19:31–34, 38; Lam 1:12

Joseph of Arimathea, who was a disciple of Jesus...asked Pilate to let him take away the body of Jesus. Pilate gave him permission; so he came and removed his body (Jn 19:31–34).

Is it nothing to you, all you who pass by? Look and see if there is any sorrow like my sorrow (Lam 1:12).

Mary, my *hope,* from the hall of Pontius Pilate to the last cry of Jesus on the cross, you had followed your Son in the grim procession to Calvary. Now you held your Son in your arms, your memory filled with the horror of the last twelve hours. How many times did you ask yourself, "Will this ever end?" I feel that you understand when I throw at God this same question, "Will this ever end?" How long must *my* passion continue? Mary, hope of the sorrowing, walk with me through my passion to the end.

THE SEVENTH SORROW

Jesus Is Laid in the Tomb

Mt 27:59; Jn 19:38–42; Mk 15:46; Lk 27:55–56

They took the body of Jesus and wrapped it with the spices in linen cloths, according to the burial custom of the Jews. Now there was a garden in the place where he was crucified, and in the garden there was a new tomb in which no one had ever been laid (Jn 29:38–42).

Mary, my *Mother,* you know well the long Holy Saturdays of life when the Love of your life was buried and the earth waited in restless wonderment for the dawn. Calvary was not the end of the suffering of your Son. Your motherhood continues in our living out of his passion. Each of us lives out a particular mystery of his passion: for some it is Jesus' utter humiliation, for others it is physical pain, for still others it is abandonment. Stay with me, Mother of the afflicted, that I may surrender myself in trust to this mystery you knew so well. I place all my hope in Jesus. Amen.

10

Praying the Mysteries of Light In Times of Darkness

By Denise Cecilia Benjamin, FSP

"I am the light of the world. Whoever follows me will never walk in darkness but will have the light of life."

—*John 8:12*

*The whole point of this life is the healing of the
heart's eye through which God is seen.*

The Talmud

The theme of "light" has been most meaningful to me, especially in my prayer life. Passages from Scripture such as, "The LORD is my light and my salvation" (Ps 27), "In your light we see light" (Ps 36), and songs like "Christ Be Our Light" touch me in a special way and move me to feel uplifted and hope-filled.

In October, 2002, Pope John Paul II surprised us all by adding to the traditional fifteen mysteries of the Rosary five new mysteries which he called the "Luminous Mysteries," or "Mysteries of Light." These new mysteries are a special gift to me, for they speak profoundly of the presence of Christ as "light" of my life.

As you pray these Mysteries of Light, may you, too, be continually reminded of the words of Jesus, "I am the Light of the world," and "I am with you always."

FIRST MYSTERY OF LIGHT

The Baptism of Jesus in the Jordan

I read...

Matthew 3:13–17

Suddenly the heavens were opened to him and he saw the Spirit of God descending like a dove and alighting on him. And a voice from heaven said, "This is my Son, the Beloved, with whom I am well pleased" (Mt 3:16–17).

I am especially struck by the words...

"...this is my beloved Son, in whom I am well pleased."

I imagine myself...

...in the water with Jesus...

I reflect:

By his own plunging into the waters of the Jordan, where sinners had come to be baptized, Jesus chose to be totally identified with everything in *my* life—the murkiness of my sins, my weakness and failures, my feelings of emptiness. He understands my human condition, and is right there with me in the darkness. And when I feel unworthy or alienated, the voice of his Father speaks also to me: "You are my beloved.... I am pleased with you.... I love you.... I have chosen you."

I pray:

Jesus, in my Baptism the light of the candle was a sign that you would forever be the light of my life. Help me to believe that you are with me in every moment of my life and in every struggle—especially in times of darkness—even if I do not see or feel this. May I hold on to that firm faith that you have promised to be with me always. Help me to remember always that I belong entirely to you, and that I am the "beloved of the Father," his "chosen one," in whom he is "well pleased."

SECOND MYSTERY OF LIGHT

The First Miracle of Jesus at the Wedding Feast of Cana

I read...

John 2:1–11

Jesus said to them, "Fill the jars with water." And they filled them up to the brim. He said to them, "Now draw some out, and take it to the chief steward" (Jn 2:7–8).

I am especially struck by the words...

"...fill these jars to the brim..."

I imagine myself...

...as one of the waiters at this wedding feast...

I reflect:

There is so much determination in the words of this woman, who says to do whatever her Son tells me. I am urged to look beyond mere appearances, to look with eyes of faith in what God can do. Sometimes my life, too, can seem like ordinary water—colorless and tasteless. But Jesus asks me to bring all of that to him—"filled to the brim." He asks me to give everything to him, and then he will change it. He said, "I make all things new," and the "pouring out" of myself before him changes me into "good wine."

I pray:

Jesus, through Mary's words, "do whatever he tells you," I am invited to let myself be transformed by you under the gaze of your Mother. Give me a real desire and resolve to give you everything—even when I feel so worthless—and to pour myself out before you, believing that you will make me new again. The water in the jars, upon being poured out, saw the light of your face and turned to wine. In my own times of darkness, help me to see you as my Light, and to truly believe that you can change the "water" of my life into "choice wine."

THIRD MYSTERY OF LIGHT

Jesus Proclaims His Kingdom of Love and Mercy

I read...

Matthew 4:12–17

The people who sat in darkness have seen a great light, and for those who sat in the region and shadow of death light has dawned (Mt 4:16).

I am especially struck by the words...

"The people who sat in darkness have seen a great light."

I imagine myself...

...as one sitting on the outskirts of the crowd, watching the Master pass by...

I reflect:

Here I am, a bruised and wounded person, perhaps shunned or rejected by others. Yet, as he stops before me, the Master is looking straight into my eyes. His face seems to be aglow, and his words are piercing my heart. He says that his kingdom is one of love and mercy, of forgiveness and healing. His is a message of justice and peace. I feel myself being warmed by his gaze. My own sufferings, both physical and spiritual, as well as my feelings of guilt or worthlessness, find new meaning in the light of these words. This gentle Galilean invites me to follow him by a life of love, forgiveness, and humble service. As I say yes to him, a tremendous hope and a deep peace fill my soul.

I pray:

Jesus, you are the light of our darkened world. As I draw near to you in humble trust, I ask you to teach me your way and lead me on the straight path. May your message of love and mercy truly find a home in my heart and uplift me when I am depressed. Forgive me for the times I have allowed my feelings of hopelessness to dampen my love for you. Strengthen me in my efforts to love everyone—even my enemies—to forgive without limits, and to be a bearer of peace. Through my witness of a life of hope in the midst of darkness, may you use me to be a light to others who do not yet know you and have not heard your good news.

FOURTH MYSTERY OF LIGHT

The Transfiguration of Jesus

I read...

Luke 9:28–35

"Master, it is good for us to be here; let us make three dwellings, one for you, one for Moses, and one for Elijah." While [Peter] was saying this, a cloud came and overshadowed them; and they were terrified as they entered the cloud. Then from the cloud came a voice that said, "This is my Son, my Chosen; listen to him!" (Lk 9:33–35)

I am especially struck by the words...

"...His face changed in appearance and his clothing became dazzling white."

I imagine myself...

...as one of the apostles with Jesus on Mount Tabor...

I reflect:

We have trekked through the harsh and rocky Palestinian terrain, and Jesus' face is usually weathered and dry, his garments dusty and brown. But now his face is radiant and his clothes brilliant. No bleacher could ever get them that white! As I gaze on him now, I am struck with awe and wonder. It gives me such joy, hope, and courage to see his glory revealed in this way. I want to hold on to this moment forever.

As I look upon him wrapped in light, I hear the Master inviting me to see beyond the dryness and muck of my life. Again I hear the Father's voice reassuring me: "This is my chosen Son. Listen to him."

I pray:

Jesus, may I never be frightened by times of depression, when clouds cast a shadow over me and sometimes blur the vision of my faith. Help me to recall and savor those times in the past when I sensed your presence so strongly and felt uplifted and consoled by your nearness. May I always hold on to the memory revealed by that glimpse of your glory. In times of trial or suffering, remind me that I have promised to follow you all the way to Calvary. You have promised me that if I die with you, I will rise with you, and you give me a foretaste of the glory of your resurrected body. In this light I am made whole, and I am strengthened with hope and joy.

FIFTH MYSTERY OF LIGHT

Jesus Gives Us Himself in the Eucharist

I read...

Luke 22:14–20

"This is my body, which is given for you. Do this in remembrance of me." And he did the same with the cup after supper, saying, "This cup that is poured out for you is the new covenant in my blood" (Lk 22:19–20).

I am especially struck by the words...

"...I have eagerly desired to eat this Passover with you...."

I imagine myself...

...as the beloved disciple next to Jesus at the table...

I reflect:

As I rest my head on the heart of the Master, I feel it beating rapidly. I sense his fear and sorrow over his impending agony and death. But I am also consoled by the depth of his desire to be with me. Jesus, too, experienced the pain of rejection, the sense of abandonment, and the torment of darkness.

But, before dying, he instituted the Eucharist, the sacrament that brings healing, strength, and comfort, because it is his own body and blood that we receive in Holy Communion. Through this sacrament he fulfills his promise to remain with us always.

I pray:

Jesus, help me to believe always more deeply in your "Real Presence" in the Holy Eucharist. United to you, may my life be transformed with the light of your love. In times of darkness, loneliness, and pain, may I trust in your desire to stay with me and your promise to never leave us orphans. Nourished by you, may I then become "bread broken for others," and share the light of your love with a hungry, darkened world.

11

For Family and Friends

"We anguish as we hear their sadness and pain."

—*Gordon and Pat*

Out of clutter, find simplicity.
Albert Einstein

Prayers

*M*y Father and my God,

I turn to you in quiet confidence. I pray by the power of your Holy Spirit that you lift my loved one from the abyss of deepening depression. Return to him the colors of your joy! Father, at creation you separated the light from darkness. I ask you to create that light within his life once more. Give unto him eyes that see with your Spirit that all is well with you. Let the shadows that now enfold him be cast away by the power of the cross of my Lord and Savior Jesus. My Lord, intercede where he cannot. I ask this because of your love and faithfulness. Amen.

Karen

Mother of God,
you witnessed your Son's suffering as you
walked his way to Calvary.
We, too, watch those we love carry heavy burdens.
Like you, we *listen, feel, support,* and *GRIEVE.*
We anguish as we hear the sadness and pain
in their voices;
see their fear and their tears, their isolation
and deadening inertia.

O comforter of the afflicted,
increase our own understanding of their suffering,
lift from their shoulders the darkness that envelops them—
darkness that freezes the mind and numbs the
heart.

But, if it be your Son's will that they find no
healing,

help them, O Mary, to see in their suffering
a *splinter* of your dear Son's Sacrificial Offering of *LOVE*.
May they—in their brokenness—find Jesus
 who was broken for them,
and may he lead them gently to himself.

Gordon and Pat

———❧———

*L*ord God, we turn to you from prison. As I listen to the inmates, to their questions, "Why do we hurt ourselves? Why did we do the things we did? Why do we hurt our loved ones?" I see them sink deeper into depression, unable to deal with their feelings when reality sinks in. Show them the way, give them the answers to help them leave this place, to find a new, more fulfilling life with you as their center.

Christine

*T*here are times when life appears to be filled
   with uncertainties,
making it difficult for us to determine what is
   going to happen next.
Please, dear God, help us handle whatever life
   sends our way.
Strengthen us with your patience,
fill our hearts and minds with
      courage, faith, and simple peace,
      as time will restore our spirit.
If we refuse to stretch ourselves,
we will never realize how far we are
      meant to reach.
If I could take all the world's fears and wor-
   ries in my arms and release them to the
   scattering winds, I would.
Dear God, help me to remember to hold on
   to hope and faith, and lean on those who
   love us for strength.

   Mary

*I*s depression contagious, Lord? I don't ever remember feeling like this before...at least not so intensely or for so long a time. Yet how can I *not* feel sad, helpless, misunderstood by others— sometimes even close to despairing—as I see my aged and infirm parents go from bad to worse? It's a thousand times more painful to watch the ones I love most suffer than to suffer myself. And when they are depressed, my Lord, how can I not be? They're terrified of being "put away" in a nursing home. I couldn't do that to them, but I'm tired and running out of energy. I even feel guilty sometimes for not having done enough when there's really nothing more that I could have done. Please, Lord, let me trust you! Show me what to do. Help me to believe that my parents and I are in your loving hands. Let me rest there in confidence and peace, knowing that you'll never abandon us.

Jamie

*I*n my office across the room
sits someone in so much pain, such despair,
such a feeling of hopelessness.
Sometimes, as a therapist, I feel hopeless
and overwhelmed by all the sadness.

But together, God, I know, we can help this
    person heal.
Help me, O God.
Enter this sacred space of relationship
between helper and one who needs healing.

Help me sit with your beloved in silence,
bearing witness to all they have suffered.
Help me listen to all of their pain.
Let the gift of your words flow through me,
    dear God.
Show me how to comfort, to soothe, and to
    help them feel your love.
With your grace, let me be an instrument of
    healing.

Let this room become a sanctuary
where hearts can soften and love can heal.

Pamela

———❧———

*J*esus, please help me during the incarceration of my son. Send your angels to guard and protect him and keep him safe in prison.

Give me the courage to hold my head up during the gossip, media coverage, and through the court procedures. Let my son know I will always be here for him; give him stamina and courage during these difficult times.

Jesus, I need you to carry him during his days, months, and years in prison, and I thank you for "one set of footprints." Your love and forgiveness will see us through until he returns home again.

Sophie

*Make room for all that which is capable of rejoicing,
enlarging, or calming your heart.*
Dietrich Bonhoeffer

As I watch the struggle, feeling helpless,
as I watch her feeling alone,
both of us knowing there is nothing I can do
    to end the pain,
Lord, help her to get through the day.
Help to make each day better than the day
    before.
Let her know that we care, and that she is not
    alone.
Help her to understand that she will get by
    the pain.

Watch over those that may have lost hope,
or may at some time reach that point.
Help them to feel not only your unconditional
    love,
but the love of those around them.
Let them know we care now and always will.

Paul

*H*ow can I reach this teenager of mine?
Overnight it seems he has entered a dark,
    dark, place
where the light of my love cannot reach.
I try and try to talk to him,
to pull him up out of the depths of his
    despair,
out of his negative thinking,
out of this sickness called depression,
but he wants to sleep all the time, and is angry
and oh, so very sad.
Dearest God, show me how to be supportive,
how to listen when I need to listen.
Give me the words,
I don't know the right words!
Dear God, please, please help him get well,
I am so frightened.
Please let my teen know that we love him.
Please bring my child back home to the light.

Parent of a teen

*L*ord,

I understand injustice more deeply today.

I heard some news that makes me sad.

Misinterpretations can lead to harsh judgments.

Misguided choices can have painful consequences.

I'm alone now.

I am here to bear the weight of sorrow.

You accepted *your* darkest moments, and I want to remain, still, in this darkness to pray.

Let me be like Mary and feel the pain that empathy brings.

Let me be like Simon of Cyrene and help to carry another's load.

Let me be like you who transform the pain and fear of dying into hope and courage, making all things new.

Donna

Healing Words to Share

You are good. You are beautiful. You are filled with the light of God.

— ❧ —

God will not let you go. He is holding you tight in his hands.

— ❧ —

Depression is an illness; it is not a punishment. God cries with you.

— ❧ —

Though you cannot see Jesus, he is carrying you over the sand. Someday you will look back and realize he was here.

*B*e gentle with yourself.

———⌒———

*T*ogether we can pray our way through this. I will stand by you.

———⌒———

*Y*ou are worthwhile. You are beautiful. God is pleased with you.

———⌒———

*G*od's love surrounds you with all the warmth and security you need.

———⌒———

*T*he healing power of God is at work within you even now.

*J*esus catches all your tears in his heart. He is with you through this. Jesus is walking with you.

———e———

*T*here will be a light at the end of this present tunnel of darkness.

———e———

I am holding up the lamp of faith for you now. I will carry this light for you as long as it is needed—until you are ready to carry it again for yourself.

Selected Bibliography

Chervin, Ronda de Sola. *Quotable Saints.* Ann Arbor: Servant Publications, 1992.

Klug, Lyn. *A Forgiving Heart: Prayers for Blessings and Reconciliation.* Minneapolis: Augsburg Books, 2003.

Koenig-Bricker, Woodeen. *Praying with the Saints.* Chicago: Loyola Press, 2001.

Mosse, Barbara. *The Treasures of Darkness.* Norwich: Canterbury Press, 2003.

O'Sullivan, Owen. *Daily Prayers for the People of God.* Boston: Pauline Books & Media, 2000.

Perrotta, Louise. *Live Jesus! Wisdom from Saints Francis de Sales and Jane de Chantal.* Ijamsville: The Word Among Us Press, 2000.

The Living Bible, owned by assignment by KNT Charitable Trust, 1971.

6 20/A a door black car

Acknowledgments

Claret, Saint Anthony Mary. From *Saint Anthony Mary Claret,* by José Maria Vinas, CMF. Copyright © 1976, Claretian Publications. Reprinted with permission of Claretian Publications, www.claretianpubs.org, 800-328-6515.

Micklem, Caryl. From *Contemporary Prayers for Public Worship,* edited by Caryl Micklem, p. 48. Copyright © 1967, SCM Press. Used with permission.

Morley, Janet. From *All Desires Known,* by Janet Morley. Copyright © 1992, SPCK. Used with permission of SPCK and Morehouse Publishing.

Kathryn James Hermes, FSP, is a member of the Congregation of the Daughters of St. Paul. She directs their Electronic Publishing Department at Pauline Books & Media, and is the author of *Beginning Contemplative Prayer; Surviving Depression: A Catholic Approach; The Journey Within: Prayer as a Path to God;* and co-author of *The Rosary: Contemplating the Face of Christ.* She holds an M.T.S. from Weston Jesuit School of Theology.

BOOKS & MEDIA

The Daughters of St. Paul operate book and media centers at the following addresses. Visit, call or write the one nearest you today, or find us on the World Wide Web, www.pauline.org

CALIFORNIA

3908 Sepulveda Blvd, Culver City, CA 90230 310-397-8676

2650 Broadway Street, Redwood City, CA 94063 650-369-4230

5945 Balboa Avenue, San Diego, CA 92111 858-565-9181

FLORIDA

145 S.W. 107th Avenue, Miami, FL 33174 305-559-6715

HAWAII

1143 Bishop Street, Honolulu, HI 96813 808-521-2731

Neighbor Islands call: 866-521-2731

ILLINOIS

172 North Michigan Avenue, Chicago, IL 60601 312-346-4228

LOUISIANA

4403 Veterans Memorial Blvd, Metairie, LA 70006 504-887-7631

MASSACHUSETTS

885 Providence Hwy, Dedham, MA 02026 781-326-5385

MISSOURI

9804 Watson Road, St. Louis, MO 63126 314-965-3512

NEW JERSEY

561 U.S. Route 1, Wick Plaza, Edison, NJ 08817 732-572-1200

NEW YORK

150 East 52nd Street, New York, NY 10022 212-754-1110

PENNSYLVANIA

9171-A Roosevelt Blvd, Philadelphia, PA 19114 215-676-9494

SOUTH CAROLINA

243 King Street, Charleston, SC 29401 843-577-0175

TENNESSEE

4811 Poplar Avenue, Memphis, TN 38117 901-761-2987

TEXAS

114 Main Plaza, San Antonio, TX 78205 210-224-8101

VIRGINIA

1025 King Street, Alexandria, VA 22314 703-549-3806

CANADA

3022 Dufferin Street, Toronto, ON M6B 3T5 416-781-9131

¡También somos su fuente para libros, videos y música en español!